COLLECTION EDITOR
**JENNIFER GRÜNWALD**
EDITORIAL ASSISTANTS
**JAMES EMMETT &
JOE HOCHSTEIN**
ASSISTANT EDITORS
**ALEX STARBUCK &
NELSON RIBEIRO**
EDITOR, SPECIAL PROJECTS
**MARK D. BEAZLEY**

SENIOR EDITOR, SPECIAL PROJECTS
**JEFF YOUNGQUIST**
SENIOR VICE PRESIDENT OF SALES
**DAVID GABRIEL**
SVP OF BRAND PLANNING & COMMUNICATIONS
**MICHAEL PASCIULLO**
BOOK DESIGN
**JEFF POWELL**

EDITOR IN CHIEF
**AXEL ALONSO**
CHIEF CREATIVE OFFICER
**JOE QUESADA**
PUBLISHER
**DAN BUCKLEY**
EXECUTIVE PRODUCER
**ALAN FINE**

**NEW MUTANTS: UNFINISHED BUSINESS.** Contains material originally published in magazine form as NEW MUTANTS #25-28. First printing 2011. Hardcover ISBN# 978-0-7851-5230-9. Softcover ISBN# 978-0-7851-5231-6. Published by MARVEL WORLDWIDE, INC., a subsidiary of MARVEL ENTERTAINMENT, LLC. OFFICE OF PUBLICATION: 135 West 50th Street, New York, NY 10020. Copyright © 2011 and 2012 Marvel Characters, Inc. All rights reserved. Hardcover: $19.99 per copy in the U.S. and $21.99 in Canada (GST #R127032852). Softcover: $16.99 per copy in the U.S. and $18.99 in Canada (GST #R127032852). Canadian Agreement #40668537. All characters featured in this issue and the distinctive names and likenesses thereof, and all related indicia are trademarks of Marvel Characters, Inc. No similarity between any of the names, characters, persons, and/or institutions in this magazine with those of any living or dead person or institution is intended, and any such similarity which may exist is purely coincidental. **Printed in the U.S.A.** ALAN FINE, EVP - Office of the President, Marvel Worldwide, Inc. and EVP & CMO Marvel Characters B.V.; DAN BUCKLEY, Publisher & President - Print, Animation & Digital Divisions; JOE QUESADA, Chief Creative Officer; JIM SOKOLOWSKI, Chief Operating Officer; DAVID BOGART, SVP of Business Affairs & Talent Management; TOM BREVOORT, SVP of Publishing; C.B. CEBULSKI, SVP of Creator & Content Development; DAVID GABRIEL, SVP of Publishing Sales & Circulation; MICHAEL PASCIULLO, SVP of Brand Planning & Communications; JIM O'KEEFE, VP of Operations & Logistics; DAN CARR, Executive Director of Publishing Technology; SUSAN CRESPI, Editorial Operations Manager; ALEX MORALES, Publishing Operations Manager; STAN LEE, Chairman Emeritus. For information regarding advertising in Marvel Comics or on Marvel.com, please contact John Dokes, SVP Integrated Sales and Marketing, at jdokes@marvel.com. For Marvel subscription inquiries, please call 800-217-9158. **Manufactured between 8/29/2011 and 9/26/2011 (hardcover), and 8/29/2011 and 3/26/2012 (softcover), by R.R. DONNELLEY, INC., SALEM, VA, USA.**

10 9 8 7 6 5 4 3 2 1

# New Mutants
## Unfinished Business

WRITERS
**DAN ABNETT & ANDY LANNING**

ARTIST, #25-27
**LEANDRO FERNANDEZ**

PENCILS, #28
**MICHAEL RYAN**

INKS, #28
**NORMAN LEE**

COLORS, #25-27
**ANDRES MOSSA**

COLORS, #28
**DAVID CURIEL**

LETTERER
**VC'S JOE CARAMAGNA**

EVEN A *FRAGMENT* IS DANGEROUS. *RECONSTRUCTING* IS WHAT IT DOES.

THIS THING--

READY FOR THE NEXT ONE?

TRIANGLE...

HI.

YOU BROUGHT FACE TO UTOPIA.

HE'S GOING TO TAKE A LOT OF CARE. JUST CONNECTING IS HARD.

AND SUPERVISION. HE'S--

"BRING HIM HOME."

MANHATTAN.

HIS NIGHTS ARE SPENT NOT SLEEPING.

HIS DAYS ARE SPENT TRYING TO PLOT A ROUTE OUT OF THIS WORLD.

HE DOESN'T LIKE IT HERE. HERE DOESN'T LIKE HIM.

"WHAT HE'S REALLY LOOKING FOR."

WHY *HERE?*

NATE GREY'S LAST KNOWN WHEREABOUTS WERE WITH OSBORN AND *H.A.M.M.E.R.*

THIS WAS *OSBORN CENTRAL* BEFORE THE WHEELS CAME OFF AND EVERYONE SAW HIM FOR THE *NUTCAKE* HE TRULY WAS.

I GOTTA ASK...DO WE REALLY *WANNA* FIND NATE GREY?

THAT'S THE ASSIGNMENT CYCLOPS GAVE US.

FEELS A LITTLE LIKE THIS TEAM IS JUST *CLEANING UP* AFTER THE SENIORS.

UNFINISHED BUSINESS.

IT'S BETTER *FINISHED*, BOBBY. IT'S THE *ONE* IMPORTANT THING THE X-MEN SHOULD HAVE BEEN DOING AS THEY WENT ALONG.

TOO MANY SKELETONS, TOO MANY CUPBOARDS, TOO MANY *NASTY SURPRISES* COMING BACK TO HAUNT US.

I *GUESS.*

BUT NATE GREY'S LIKE *FREAKY POWERFUL* AND STUFF. THE DUDE'S *SCARY.*

DO WE *REALLY* WANT TO MESS WITH HIM?

HE'S ONE OF US. THAT'S *ALL* THAT MATTERS.

I'VE *FOUND* SOMETHING.

A CLUE, DOUG?

WE'RE NOT "X-KIDS," WE--

MY TEAM DOESN'T WANT TO CAUSE A *PROBLEM*, SIR.

IT'S *ALREADY* PRETTY CLEAR THIS ISN'T WHERE WE NEED TO LOOK.

JUST HAD TO CROSS IT *OFF* THE LIST.

GOOD LUCK WITH YOUR SEARCH.

GOOD LUCK WITH THIS SITE.

MISS HAND, GOOD LUCK WITH THE PERSONALITY.

ARE WE *REALLY* LEAVING?

WELL, IT'S A DEAD END, PLUS, IF WE'D STAYED ANY LONGER, I WOULD HAVE PUNCHED A GOVERNMENT OFFICIAL, AND *THAT* WOULDN'T HAVE ENDED WELL.

OH, OKAY.

IT'S JUST THAT THIS *IS* THE PLACE.

SO, RONNY. READY?

WHAT DO I HAVE TO DO?

I'M GOING TO OPEN A DOOR, RONNY. YOU GO *THROUGH*, TELL ME WHAT'S ON THE *OTHER* SIDE.

IS THAT *ALL?*

REALLY QUICK, REALLY *SIMPLE.*

WAIT HERE WHILE I SET UP.

IF YOU CAN, YOU SHOULD GET *OUT* OF HERE.

HUH?

W-WHO ARE YOU?

DOES THAT *HURT?*

YEAH, IT *HURTS.* I CAN'T GET OUT.

THIS IS THE OMEGA MACHINE, AND I'M *STUCK* IN IT.

WHAT'S AN OMEGA MACHINE?

LOOK AT THE WRITING. THE *GRAFFITI.*

LIKE ANY *OTHER* DEAD LOT.

SOME OF IT'S JUST *VANDALISM.* SOME OF IT'S *TAGGING.*

THERE'S *WILDSTYLE,* WHICH IS PRETTY *HARD* TO EXTRACT MEANING FROM.

BUT THERE'S *CODE* HERE TOO.

CODE, SELF-FRIEND?

YOU EVER HEAR OF THE *HOBO CODE?*

IT'S A SYSTEM OF SYMBOLS EVOLVED TO HELP THE HOMELESS COMMUNITY.

INFORMATION, WARNINGS, DIRECTIONS.

THE CODE CAN TELL A HOBO WHERE HE COULD GET *FOOD,* OR FIND A *FRIENDLY HOUSE,* WHERE THERE MIGHT BE WORK...

...OR WHERE THE COPS WERE *ROUGH,* OR THERE WAS A *MEAN* YARD-DOG.

SOMEONE'S BEEN LEAVING *CODE MARKS* HERE, FOR PEOPLE WHO *KNOW* TO LOOK FOR THEM.

YOU'VE GOT TO KNOW *WHERE* TO LOOK, AND *WHAT* TO LOOK FOR.

AND YOU'VE GOT TO *WANT* TO FIND WHAT THEY'RE LEADING YOU TO.

WHICH IS *WHAT?*

27

NATHAN? *NATE?*

WE'RE X-MEN FROM UTOPIA. WE'RE HERE TO *RESCUE* YOU.

X-MEN...

DO NOT STRUGGLE, NEWFRIEND--

WHAT IS THIS THING? WHAT HAVE THEY STRAPPED HIM *INTO?*

SOULFRIEND DOUG, THIS MECHANISM IS *NEURAL* BONDED.

DETACHING= EXTREME RISK.

HE'S BEEN WIRED INTO IT FOR MONTHS. HE'S *MUTANT* FUEL TO KEEP IT STOKED.

IT CHANNELS HIS MUTANT POWERS TO WARP *REALITY* AND OPEN DOORS TO *OTHER* PLACES.

IT HURTS SO MUCH.

HE WAS OSBORN'S PLAYTHING BEFORE THE FALL OF *H.A.M.M.E.R.*

SO WAS SUGAR MAN. WHEN THE WALLS CAME DOWN, SUGAR MAN ESCAPED FROM HIS CELL, AND FOUND THE OMEGA MACHINE IN THE RUBBLE. FOUND *NATE GREY.*

AND NATE GREY BECAME *SUGAR MAN'S* PLAYTHING INSTEAD.

HE WANTS TO TELL THEM IT'S CALLED *THE OMEGA MACHINE.* OSBORN FUSED HIM TO IT.

HE WANTS TO TELL THEM, BUT HIS MOUTH CAN'T MANAGE ALL THE WORDS.

WE'LL TAKE THIS *SUGAR MAN* INTO CUSTODY.

BE CAREFUL. HE'S *VERY* DANGEROUS.

UTOPIA WILL PROVIDE A FULL AND *ANNOTATED* CASE FILE OF *SPECIES CRIMES* YOU MAY WANT TO CONSIDER IN RELATION TO HIS ACTIVITIES.

THESE KIDS WILL NEED CARE AND TREATMENT *TOO.*

THEIR UPGRADES MUST BE REMOVED AS *SOON* AS POSSIBLE.

WHAT CONCERNS *ME* IS THE ONE WHO WAS *DOING* ALL THIS REALITY WARPING.

WE'LL DEFINITELY BE TAKING *HIM* INTO CUSTODY FOR--

NO. HE'S COMING WITH US.

AND MY DAD'S BIGGER THAN *YOUR* DAD. BLAH.

AND I HAVE *MINE.*

A REALITY-WARPING MUTANT IS A MATTER OF *INTERNATIONAL* SECURITY.

I HAVE MY ORDERS.

COMMANDER, ROGERS, NATE GREY IS A MEMBER OF THE *SUMMERS* FAMILY.

VICTORIA, CONSIDER YOUR ORDERS *REVISED*.

A *REALITY-WARPING* MUTANT--

IS *X-MEN* BUSINESS.

THANK YOU, SIR. HE IS ALSO NO *LONGER* A THREAT. IT LOOKS LIKE HIS *POWER'S GONE. BURNED OUT.*

MS. MOONSTAR, PLEASE TELL SCOTT MY THOUGHTS ARE WITH THIS... *RELATIVE* OF HIS.

I HOPE HE RECOVERS *QUICKLY*.

HIS *HEALTH*. HE *MEANS* HIS *HEALTH*.

GOOD JOB, BY THE WAY.

WELL, IF IT ISN'T THE FAMOUS DANI MOONSTAR.

THANKS FOR INVITING ME HERE. PROMISE I'LL BE ON MY BEST BEHAVIOR.

THANKS FOR COMING.

AND BELIEVE ME I DON'T WANT YOUR BEST BEHAVIOR. I WANT YOUR...REGULAR BEHAVIOR.

GOD, NO ONE WANTS THAT. USUALLY ENDS UP BLOODY.

I WANT BLOODY. I WANT YOU TO GO FOR THE THROAT.

DO YOU REALLY? I DON'T KNOW HOW USEFUL I'M GOING TO BE TO YOU, MIND.

WE'RE LIKELY DEALING WITH A RANGE OF SPECIFIC ISSUES I FRANKLY HAVE NO EXPERIENCE OF.

WE'RE ALL PEOPLE.

THAT'S THE TRUTH.

"HE APPEARS TO BE BOTH A COWBOY AND AN INDIAN."

THE PREFERRED TERM IS NATIVE AMERICAN.

HIS NAME IS GUS GRIM.

THEN HE APPEARS TO BE BOTH A COWBOY AND AN INDIAN *AND* HE HAS A STUPID NAME.

HE'S A COGNITIVE THERAPIST FROM COLORADO. DANI KNEW HIM YEARS AGO.

HE USED TO WORK IN THE CHEYENNE COMMUNITIES.

LIKE A *SOCIAL WORKER?*

I SUPPOSE.

SO THIS IS A VISIT FROM AN OLD FRIEND?

NO. HE'S HERE TO WORK WITH THE MORE *DAMAGED* MEMBERS OF HER TEAM.

AS A THERAPIST? *AS A THERAPIST?*

THIS IS DANI'S CALL.

YOU LET HER BRING IN AN *EXTERNAL THERAPIST?*

IT'S IMPORTANT I SUPPORT HER COMMAND DECISIONS.

SHE WANTED SOMEONE *IMPARTIAL.* I THINK SHE'S CONSCIOUS OF HOW *INCESTUOUS* OUR COMMUNITY IS SOMETIMES.

BUT HE'S...

PLEASE DON'T SAY HE'S "NOT ONE OF US" BECAUSE WE KNOW HOW POSITIVE *THAT* PHILOSOPHY CAN BE.

1

YOU STEPPED DOWN AS TEAM LEADER. DANI MOONSTAR TOOK YOUR PLACE.

TEAM COULDN'T BE IN *BETTER* HANDS.

THEY COULD BE IN *YOUR* HANDS.

I'VE REVIEWED MISSION PROFILES. THE PERIOD KNOWN AS *AGE OF X*, YOU *EXCELLED* AS FIELD LEADER OF THE X-MEN.

I DON'T WANT TO TALK ABOUT THAT.

NEITHER DO I. I'VE GOT *ONE* DAY HERE. *LOTS* TO COVER.

I DON'T HAVE TIME TO WASTE *CHATTING*.

WOW. GREAT ATTITUDE, *MR. THERAPIST*.

WHINE ABOUT MY APPROACH WHEN I'M *NOT* HERE TO LISTEN.

*FOCUS*.

IT'S TOUGH TO UNTANGLE *P.T.S.D.* FROM FEELINGS OF *GUILT*. THAT'S A *BASIC FACT*.

THERE'S *TRAUMA*, AND THERE'S A *RELUCTANCE* TO *EXPOSE* YOURSELF TO THAT TRAUMA.

SO I'VE GOT POST-TRAUMATIC STRESS DISORDER?

MAN, I HOPE SO, OTHERWISE THIS IS JUST *SELF-INDULGENT*.

YOU ARE & % * $ % & UNBELIEVABLE!

ANGER. OKAY.

AT LAST, AN ACTUAL *EMOTION* SHOWS UP.

YOU RESIGNED AS TEAM LEADER. YOU PLACED YOURSELF IN A *SECURE WARD*, AND REQUESTED *PSYCHIATRIC OBSERVATION*.

WELL, HERE IT IS. THIS IS WHAT YOU *ASKED* FOR.

SO SHUT UP AND LISTEN.

YOU KNOW THAT BECAUSE YOU'RE A TELEPATH AND YOU'RE IN HIS HEAD?

HIS ONLY MEANS OF ARTICULATION IS TO EXPRESS CHRONIC FRUSTRATION BY VIOLENTLY DISCHARGING ENERGY, MR. GRIM.

HE EXISTS IN A WORLD HE CANNOT ENGAGE WITH.

MY BOND WITH HIM PROVIDES THE ONLY EXTERNALIZED INTERACTION HE CAN EVER KNOW.

HIS ONLY ROUTE FOR PERCEPTION.

SO THAT MEANS HE REALLY MAKES YOU SPECIAL, DOESN'T HE?

WHAT? WHAT?

THIS IS ONE OF THE FEW PLACES ON THE PLANET WHERE THERE ARE TELEPATHS AND EMPATHS EVERYWHERE YOU LOOK, BUT THIS HAS TO BE YOU.

WHY?

BECAUSE I CAN--

BECAUSE--

HOW DARE YOU!

I'LL LET YOU THINK ABOUT THAT.

THERE ARE OTHERS THAT COULD HELP YOU. YOU DON'T HAVE TO CARRY THIS ALONE.

SO WHY ARE YOU? TRY FORMING AN ACCURATE ANSWER THAT DOESN'T INVOLVE THE WORD "SELFISH."

PROTOCOL OF WARDING AND BANISHMENT ENACTED.

EEAAAARRGHHHHH!

THANK YOU, DANGER.

I WAS HOPING YOU WOULD TRY TO ESCAPE SO I COULD SEE IF MY RESTRAINTS WORKED.

ANOTHER TIME, MAYBE.

YOU'D BEST FETCH DANI. MR. GRIM PROBABLY NEEDS A CUP OF TEA AND A SIT-DOWN.

IT'S NOT ABOUT FRIENDS.

IN THE COMMUNITY, YOU ALWAYS DEALT WITH PROBLEMS CLEAN AND QUICK, TO MINIMIZE DAMAGE.

IF YOU EVER TOOK TIME TO BE ANYTHING OTHER THAN DIRECT, LIVES GOT HURT. OR LOST.

I'VE BEEN GIVEN A TEAM TO LEAD, GUS.

AND IT'S A MESS.

DANI, SOMETIMES PEOPLE NEED TIME TO--

WE'RE X-MEN, GUS. I THINK THAT APPROACH SUITS US.

WE WILL *NEVER* HAVE TIME TO SIT AROUND FEELING SORRY FOR OURSELVES OR NURSING WOUNDS.

WE NEED TO GET FIXED UP FAST SO WE CAN *KEEP* MOVING.

WELL, OKAY. BUT I DON'T KNOW WHAT YOU EXPECT.

I EXPECT TO SEE YOU AGAIN NEXT WEEK.

IN THE MEANTIME, WE'LL THINK ABOUT YOUR ADVICE AND SEE WHERE IT GETS US.

YOU DON'T HAVE *MUCH* IN THE WAY OF POWERS, AND YOU DON'T KNOW WHAT TO *DO* WITH THEM *ANYWAY.*

I DIDN'T HAVE ANY POWERS UNTIL RECENTLY. I WAS TRAINED TO GET BY WITHOUT.

EVEN NOW, I'M NOT *COMFORTABLE* USING THEM.

NATHAN SUMMERS SPENT ALL OF MY CHILDHOOD PREPARING ME TO FACE THE *REST* OF MY LIFE.

WOULD IT BE OKAY WITH YOU IF I TAUGHT YOU SOME OF THE THINGS HE TAUGHT ME?

I...

I'D LIKE THAT.

ROOM?

RESTART.

NEXT: *FEAR ITSELF*

#25 VARIANT
BY ARTHUR ADAMS & PETER STEIGERWALD

#25 VARIANT
BY JORGE MOLINA

#28 I AM CAPTAIN
AMERICA VARIANT

BY AUSTIN MADISON

# CHARACTER SKETCHES
## BY LEANDRO FERNANDEZ

CANNONBALL
SAM GUTHRIE

CYPHER
DOUGLAS RAMSEY

SUNSPOT
ROBERTO DA COSTA

WARLOCK

KARMA
XI'AN COY MANH

MAGIK
ILLYANA RASPUTIN

MAGMA
AMARA AQUILLA

MIRAGE
DANIELLE MOONSTAR

CANNONBALL

CANNONBALL

LEANDRO
FERNANDEZ '10

MIRAGE

MAGMA

# ALTERING THE DNA

## The New Mutants Take On A New Life With Writers Dan Abnett And Andy Lanning

By Robert Greenberger

**N**ew Mutants returned with a bang in 2009 when Zeb Wells and Diogenes Neves gave readers a fresh look at the younger members of the X-Men's cast. Amid returning friends and foes, the team has struggled to find its place in a world of barely 200 mutants.

The series will get a shot in the arm this spring with the arrival of new writers Dan Abnett and Andy Lanning. The two have been prolific through the years since their collaboration began during the 1990s, both together and on their own. Abnett is an accomplished novelist, exploring fantasy worlds for Black Flame Library; he recently sold his first original novels to the UK's Angry Robot press. As an inker, Lanning remains in demand with a lengthy list of credits over the field's biggest pencilers.

Abnett and Lanning are no strangers to epic-scale super heroics – beginning in 2000 with DC Comics' *Legion of Super-Heroes*, followed by a stint on

*New Mutants #25* cover by Marko Djurdjevic.

WildStorm's *The Authority*. But since 2008, they've made their reputations working on their largest canvas yet on Marvel's *Annihilation* cycle of titles, a revived *Guardians of the Galaxy* and more.

Abnett and Lanning explained why teams hold such appeal. "We particularly enjoy the interaction of the character dynamics. Everything is character-driven for us. It sounds like an insult, but there's a soap-opera quality that is delicious to weave."

The move to *New Mutants*, then, suits the pair just fine. "We were both kids who read and adored the classic Claremont/Byrne run, and the X-books remained favorite reads from that point."

When interviewed, Abnett and Lanning prefer to speak in one voice, as they write. "There's a particular dynamic of shared character continuity that the X-books do so well. When we first started to consider the *New Mutants* characters from a writing point of view, we found they were bizarrely familiar to us, like friends we'd known for a long time."

Wells' saga ended with issue #21, the conclusion to his "Fall of the/Rise of the New Mutants" storyline. The team was left licking its wounds after ending the threat of Project Purgatory and preventing the Elder Gods from destroying the world. The following three issues detoured into the "Age of X" crossover with *X-Men: Legacy,* and Abnett and Lanning took over with May's issue #25.

What happens when a new creative team arrives on a title? Do they start over from scratch? Build on their predecessors' work? Or just take direction from the editor? "Can we say all three? Zeb's built a great foundation for us with his run. It's like a relay race where we're taking the baton from him. We don't want to demolish everything he's set up, so there are character points and the repercussions of recent stories to deal with. Even if our style's a little different, the character linkage should be seamless from the readers' point of view. That's where (editor) Nick (Lowe) comes in. He knows what he wants, and the oversight he brings is

genuinely impressive. He's properly orchestrating the efforts of all the creative teams and can help the books — and the crisscrossing characters within them — operate without contradiction. But...he's also hired us to bring new thoughts and new ideas with us. New characters, too."

But before they could begin, they needed to make familiarize themselves with all the recent the goings-on in both the X-titles and the broader Marvel Universe. And that means "lots of reading, lots of fact-checking, lots of research. On the plus side, lots of audience, lots of invested love for these characters."

As conceived by writer Chris Claremont and artist Bob McLeod in 1982, the New Mutants were a group of teens studying to one day become X-Men. But a fair amount of Marvel time has passed since the team's first appearance, and the age gap between the New Mutants and X-Men is less of a factor today than in those original stories.

"There's not so much difference anymore," Abnett and Lanning said. "These guys don't call themselves the New Mutants. That's just the book's title. Nick was keen to stress that they are grownup, proven, graduated characters — fully one of the X-Men teams."

Having done their homework, Abnett and Lanning recognized that Wells left plenty of dangling threads for them to play with — leading them to name their opening arc "Unfinished Business." And there's plenty for the New Mutants to do. "Cyclops charges them with this specific task: to tidy loose ends that the X-Men often have no time to clean up, and which then end up biting them on the

Logan, Colossus and Kitty team up with the New Mutants squad in DnA's first issue. (Art from *NM #25* by Leandro Fernandez.)

TAKING THE OFFENSIVE: Dani Moonstar is looking badder than ever! (Art from *NM #25* by Fernandez.)

behind. It's a systematic effort to close cases and clean house, to get rid of any lingering nasty surprises. First order of business: Find Nate Grey."

Since his introduction in 1995's "Age of Apocalypse" saga, the son of Earth-295's Scott Summers and Jean Grey has struggled to find a place for himself in the Marvel Universe. He resurfaced during last year's *Siege* epic, psychically tortured within Norman Osborn's mind, which left him powerless in the corporeal world. Nate was last seen being dragged off panel during *Dark X-Men #5*, and it now falls to Abnett and Lanning to figure out what happened.

"It's hard to define Nate," they said. "Nate probably has a hard time defining himself. That's what we're going to do in this story: find out how he ticks, what he needs, where

"FIND X-MAN!": The New Mutants' first mission is to find out where in the world is Nate Grey. (Cover to *NM #25* by Jorge Molina.)

he's going. He learns about himself as we learn about him."

Nate's fate is not the only thing the team will be confronting in the opening months of Abnett and Lanning's run. Another thread to be explored is what it means to be a young teen mutant in a world with under 200 mutants. "There's a real feeling of community – or a family reduced in a time of peril who know they have to work extra hard, together, through lean years, so that the family can rebuild and thrive. There is a sense of determination," the writers said.

Any community sees people coming and going, and members stepping into the spotlight based on circumstances. As a result, Abnett and Lanning foresee making "gentle modifications" to the team's lineup. "Just a little boost in prominence for some and a chance to step back for others. Nothing traumatic. And just because a character becomes 'inactive' on the team roster for a while, it doesn't mean they won't feature in the book. Some characters' stories will be about them *not* being on the team."

Given the writers' previous work, might the team find itself rocketing to the stars? "New Mutants in space? We're still working out exactly how it's going to go, but there's got to be some cool cosmic cross-continuity we can play with."

The New Mutants have plenty of earthbound business to take care of first, but the writers warned it won't be all action. "Nick wants as much kissing as possible, so pretty much anyone is fair game. We're trying to work out the most interesting, surprising, satisfying or unexpected possibilities."

Each writer took a moment to identity his favorite New Mutant and favorite New Mutant foe with Abnett answering, "I'd be hard pressed to call it between Illyana and Cypher. The Hellions." Lanning replied, "Dani or Warlock. The Demon Bear." There are other members of the New Mutants' rogues' gallery Abnett and Lanning eagerly await bringing on stage, but they won't name names. "Answering that would be giving away some big surprises. The X-books have a great villain catalogue. There aren't many we're not excited to use. Plus, we're bringing a few new ones along."

Joining them to visualize these exciting new tales is Leandro Fernandez, who previously illustrated Garth Ennis' *Punisher MAX*. The writers heaped praise on their collaborator. "His art is wonderful and he's extremely hard-working. We're just seeing the first pages come through now, and we're open to anything he sends us in terms of ideas."

Abnett and Lanning are clearly eager to get rolling, anticipating fan reaction over the summer months. "Apart from kissing and real high drama, we hope this book is going to be fun...fun and funny, when it needs to be."

New Mutants #25, *featuring the debut of DnA in Marvel's Mutant Universe, hits stores in May!* ●